SERIAL BOOKS
Architecture & Urbanism 4

PUBLIC SPACES

CHORA / Raoul Bunschoten

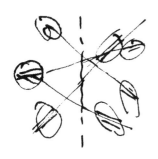

Apeiron, Berlin *8*

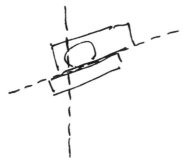

Constantini Museum, Buenos Aires *12*

Welsh National Opera, Cardiff *20*

Prado Museum, Madrid *28*

Omphalos, Ottakringer Brewery, Vienna *36*

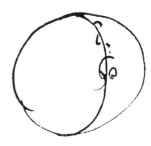

Meridian Walk, London *42*

Salamander Factory, Stuttgart Region *46*

Municipal Museum of Contemporary Art, Rome *54*

New Suburb, Høje Taastrup, Copenhagen *56*

Architectural principles

Prototypes

The word prototype calls up images of a new car or other technological object that forms a model for testing, but a prototype is also a programmatic condition: it is an organisation of programmes in a new and initially singular manner. The prototype in that case is not an object in itself, it is a device in the form of a specific architectural configuration, an organisational structure embedded in the architecture or urban space that links and intertwines programmes in such a way as to give them dynamic properties. These lead to emergent spatial, social, political and other developing qualities. The form of an embedded prototype can be diagrammatised. Often, the architectural form of the prototype is itself diagrammatic – it is an embedded diagram. Since diagrams are essentially operational devices that transform matter, that transfer qualities of one thing or situation into another thing or onto another situation, they are machines of mutation. The diagrammatic condition of prototypes relates both to their singular condition of creating a new link, an innovation as well as to what evolves from a prototype when it adapts and proliferates.

Public spaces must have a prototypical character; they are instruments of change for a society. They are singular, they create an identity, and they must be able to stimulate the evolution of all kinds of parts of a society. The singularness of public spaces remains a key attractor for a variety of people, events, collective expressions, programmes, but what comes out constantly changes, adapts to new trends,

forces, desires, and it multiplies in its adaptations over time. The use of a public space proliferates increasingly in the ways that they are used and the ways that they give form to a society and its dynamic mechanisms. The projects in this book were not necessarily conceived as prototypes, but they became the expression of a search for a combination of form and operational device that together would create the architectural space and quality. Only did it gradually become clear that in fact this combination between form – specifically diagrammatic form – and the operational mechanism of a prototype together are the link between architectural space and urban dynamics.

Since the publication of the book *Urban Flotsam* in which we developed this notion, it seemed right to take stock of the other work we had produced in Chora and concentrate on qualities that would define the public space and its role in cities more directly. During the period of work on *Urban Flotsam*, and more since that period, we have become involved in implementations of the methods demonstrated therein. These projects are under way in the Netherlands and Ireland. Despite the fact that none of these projects have been realised (the Danish project takes place in a slightly different form in the Netherlands) there is a body of work that both aims at constructing public spaces in cities, in a variety of ways – there is an urban debate in all of these projects – but they also develop an architectural vocabulary. This vocabulary relates to objects, conditions and forms that belong to a broad associative field: a field in which memories of very primary things mix with pure play and the invention of future possibilities.

I believe that there must be a method in urban design, a method that allows many parties to find an entry into the processes that make up urban form, a method that stimulates continuous change. In the most recent project, the prize winning competition entry for a new suburb, there is a method that initiates and regulates dynamic growth, a method that identifies urban prototypes and suggests the conditions in which they can become effective. The form of this project is its game board and the organisational structure of its dynamic 'drivers'. The Meridian project, conceived together with Takuro Hoshino, who was also involved in several of our other initiatives, introduces a method of development but it relies on a visible form – the Meridian – which is not built, but resides deep in the cultural and collective consciousness. It could be built however, and that is its drive. The other projects use methodical forms: intersecting lines and planes, cuts, rhythmic layers, but the language of the skin of the earth, the rock, the wave, the hill, becomes a leading trait in most of them. This becomes an opaque but associative form language which itself becomes a kind of public realm. Very simple, and deeply embodied in human consciousness.

It would be a stifling set of gestures if all projects could not incorporate an aspect of the playground. The public space is the playground of society, the public realm is the playground in which society reinvents itself. In Berlin the playground is the burnt earth on which new structures are constructed that attempt not to touch the ground too much, that seem to weave back and forth across a global and historical divide between East and West Berlin. In Cardiff the square in front of the main cut of the façade becomes the playground for new forms of music and other theatre that emerges out of the main doors of the combined stages. In Buenos Aires the playground is the square that slides underneath the permanent collection and is where the temporary exhibitions are staged. These spill over into the square, or vice versa – the urban activity staged on the square spills over into the art gallery. In Madrid, this is a carpet for the ceremony of the church and the ceremonial entry into one of the most moving art collections in the world. In Vienna the playground, festival brewery, film and theatre, and new streets, finished by a playground that is literally positioned on the top of Vienna. In Rome the playground is both the multi-programmability of the curatable spaces, and also the game board playground on top of the building, an elevated city square, reaching out to the other roofscapes of Rome and its wonderous heavens. In the Meridian project the playground shifts to the negotiation table, and to the way each zone plays with this blinding image invading their space. In the new suburb project the whole city becomes a game board, a playground for emergent phenomena, desires, new potentials, and the dynamics of the mixed life of a city. Playgrounds and public spaces need room – fields to play and act in, and objects to play with, identify with and react against. This is the architecture. The rest is city life.

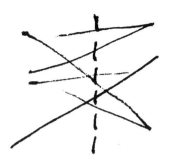

Apeiron, Berlin 8

Constantini Museum, Buenos Aires 12

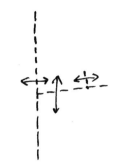

Welsh National Opera, Cardiff 20

Prado Museum, Madrid 28

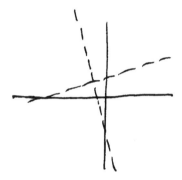

Omphalos, Ottakringer Brewery, Vienna 36

Meridian Walk, London 42

Salamander Factory, Stuttgart Region 46

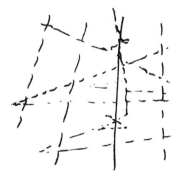

Municipal Museum of Contemporary Art, Rome 54

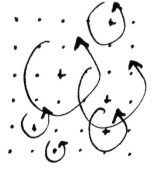

New Suburb, Høje Taastrup, Copenhagen 56

Patterns of use

Apeiron, Berlin

Apeiron was produced for an exhibition in Berlin organised by Kristin Feireiss, in 1988. The most material of all of our projects, it is a model of a complex public space that has deep historical layers and is of relevance today in the context of the recent restructuring of the Potsdamerplatz area – it is also our most ambitious project. The design and implementation of this public space could have significant political consequences. The basic premise is: ground as a public space at the centre of a state. As 'burnt ground' the site is a symbol of a regime and its actions. As separated ground the site becomes a site of conflict and confrontation, a division within a city, a frontier between states, a battle line between superpowers and global political systems. Now it is the site a of fast development and the symbol of new state power, public space as a new centre for a reunited city.

Berlin, September 1988

A boundless field of clouds passes over Berlin. The shadows of one is held in place momentarily to demarcate an area, Apeiron, an area which contained the old political centre of Germany. Apeiron is a word indicating a boundless field from which "things separate off" according to Anaxagoras, the pre-Socratic philosopher. It is a field which cannot be traversed. This boundary is called the Berlin Wall. The shadow of the cloud is initially unaffected by the typology of the ground on which it falls, but during its transfiguration from ephemeral discoloration into a substance coagulating into particles the shadow absorbs some of the aspects of the typology of the ground. It needs an identity; for that it borrows the programme of a temporal dichotomy, the

programme of a power game between two adversaries, of which the edge is a product and symptom.
The field as Annunciation: synopsis and diaeresis.
The images of the Annunciation show us how on one side two protagonists face each other in an apparently continuous space. Instead of being similar beings the protagonists become symbols for two completely different but co-existing worlds. The touching of these two worlds only becomes visible as a diagram. The Apeiron field is organised like an Annunciation: apparently continuous with seemingly similar protagonists and an almost accidentally placed construction that separates the field.

Berlin, 9 November 1989

A rupture in time, the dissolution of a boundary, the chasm in Apeiron disappears. If a dream materialises, it takes on the form and the substance of the material world. The cut within the field does not affect the autonomy of the cloud; it does, however, form a kind of origin for the materialisation of the field, a reason for its outlay. The field emerges in the outline of a play, a game – a powergame – with stones to mark positions, and cuts in the stones to direct them. These stones, particles of the field, hug a burned ground. Lines cut into the ground connect them, pathways lacing the field, suturing its edges as if closing a gap. At night these gaps light up: a discontinuous field of fragmented lines emerge signalling a new form of civic centre that is multiple and not singular.

← Model particle building. Ferro-cement panels with stitches and steel 'metacity'

singularity
a (former) rupture

APEIRON,
topology
of a cloud's shadow

particles and
anchors

APEIRON
the urban field

Particle model: a building made of new earth, a cut for light, the metacity

Suturing the Berlin Wall, Potsdamerplatz and surroundings

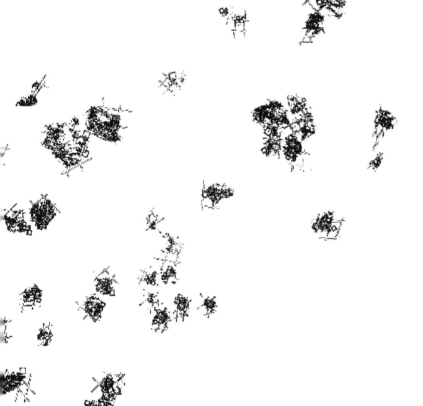

Cloud of particles, metacities and anchors

Constantini Museum for South American Art, Buenos Aires

Constantini is an art collector who has brought together a large collection of South American Art. The competition brief asked for a design that would both accommodate this collection, as well as create facilities for temporary exhibitions, lectures, a library and other public spaces. The project is located in a central location in Buenos Aires, on a square where Carlo Burle Marx had built a large central sculpture, which was demolished ten years ago. The memory of this sculpture and the clustering of other cultural institutions in the area became important factors in the design. On an urban scale the museum is anchored in the fabric of the city by a large cross with acute angles. The art collection forms a block that sits on this cross, the public facilities are situated in a beam-like structure that mediates between this block and the ground. The cross is a marker in the city centre. It also regulates pedestrian traffic across the site, from a shopping centre on one side of the square to another cultural facility on the other side, from the busy avenue on one side to the quiet quarters on the other. This cross has more functions though: it separates the square into four quadrants that each have distinct spatial qualities, moods, and public functions. The largest of these quadrants is a public square that forms a large open space in the middle of a dense city core, but a space that slides down underneath the block with the art collection. The cross creates edges and façades, it enables movement through the building, and it provides the topology for the movement within the building. The arm that provides this infrastructure slices through the two building elements. The public facilities block is tilted, it allows a path up from the square towards the art gallery floors. This building element is a public room, a liminal space, a threshold between the art gallery and the square. The square and cross form a platform for the cultural collection of Latin American Art. The square is an extension of the art collection: temporary exhibitions take place in the interior part of the square underneath the main block. The square becomes a projection place for urban activities organised by the Art Museum, city events merge with the collection on the square. The memory of Burle Marx's work crosses back over the main cut of the cross and becomes a void in the mass housing the permanent art collection.

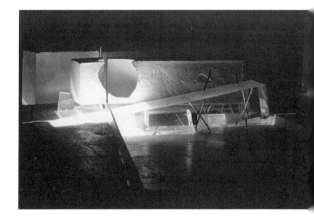

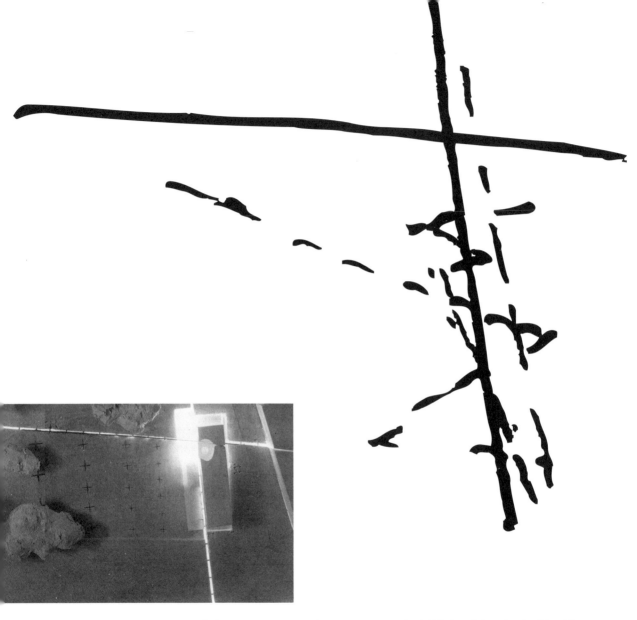

The Constantini Museum with the new public square (left) and the anchor points

Two lines crossing: one, the 'Knife' (horizontal), forms the urban link and the other, the 'Cut' (vertical), forms a plane that both divides the two main building elements as well as providing the internal infrastructure of the building

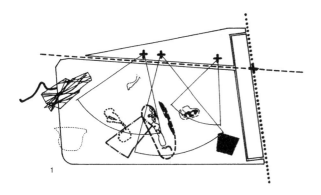

1

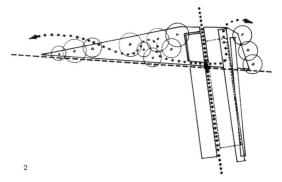

2

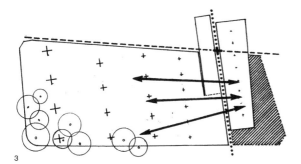

3

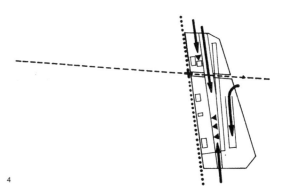

4

Quadrants surrounding the Knife and the Cut:

1 Viewing platform for events on the public square

2 Garden along the Knife, public pedestrian route to and through the museum

3 Public square with anchor points, square slips underneath and into the museum, becoming its temporary gallery space, which is an extension of the city

4 Pedestrian access into the museum and the car park entrance

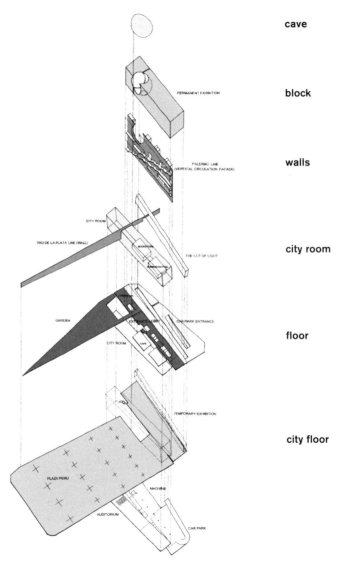

cave

block

walls

city room

floor

city floor

PERMANENT EXHIBITION

PALERMO LINE
(VERTICAL CIRCULATION. FACADE)

CITY ROOM

RIO DE LA PLATA LINE (WALL)

BOOKSTORE

THE CUT OF LIGHT

ADMINISTRATION

GARDEN

ENTRANCE LOBBY

CAR PARK ENTRANCE

CITY ROOM

CAFE

TEMPORARY EXHIBITION

PLAZA PERU

MACHINE

AUDITORIUM

CAR PARK

← View of the Constantini Museum from the new square: the Urban Room rising
from the square, suspended by 'walking columns', flanked by the the block
containing the permanent collection and large cave with the light well – a
memory of the Burle Marx sculpture that once occupied the centre of the square

Exploded view of the museum and the square

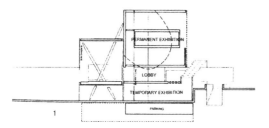

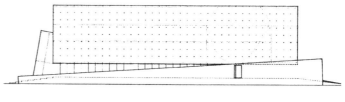

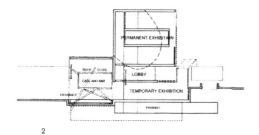

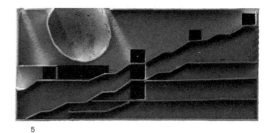

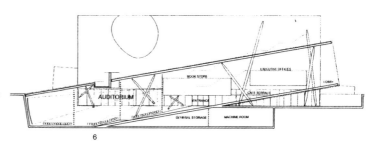

1 Section: continuity between square and the temporary gallery

2 Section: connection square and Urban Room

3 Section: auditorium, the cave that forms the light well of the lobby

4 Elevation: frosted glass wall of permanent collection

5 Section model: double staircase, cave

6 Section: Urban Room with all public facilities, rising above the connection
   between the square and the temporary art gallery

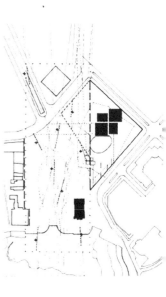

Welsh National Opera, Cardiff

The Welsh National Opera needs a new building in Cardiff. The site chosen for the competition was situated next to the old harbor, on a derelict and mostly empty piece of land. Planned development however will turn this land into a new city centre, with a public square, open to the sea, at its core. The sea embodies much of the history of this site. Sailors left from here to travel the ocean. But there is still a feeling, an imaginary presence that comes in from the sea and finds an echo in some of the music that will resonate in the cave-like spaces of the opera auditorium. The opera building has a very simple form: it fills out the available space between the street pattern, but is cut sharply on the side of the square to create a long, transparent façade defining the square. This façade is a projection surface, it is a site for art works using light, sound or other means, it speaks to the square. It is also a section through the majority of functions of the opera. From the outside you see the dress makers, practice rooms, large doors opening to the stage, the café and restaurant, the lobby. The main building is a triangular striated mass layered vertically with spaces decreasing in size towards the thin skin of the façade that faces the square. Within this base a large perambulatory rock seems to have been set – the auditorium. Carved into the top layer of the base building is a large, translucent and pneumatic roof, which has shifted slightly, offering expanded roof parts to cover the entrances. The rock projects above this roof. The stage tower becomes, above the roof, a cube, which is joined by three other cubes, the orchestra rehearsal rooms. These four cubes and the bit of rock protruding above the roof become a kind of metacity, poised on a horizon created by inclining the roof slightly towards the square. The opera is formed by a classical opera configuration with a round auditorium and a T-sized stage. The triangle is basically divided into two parts: one half for the production facilities, the other for the public. They overlap in the elongated stage space.

Contemporary music and especially new music theatre has a hard time competing with the traditional form of opera. Building new facilities for them is, mostly, not feasible. This project uses the requirements for a rehearsal stage doubling as experimental theatre and turns it into a programme for a fully equipted new music theatre riding piggyback on the larger, traditional opera. The new theatre is a rectangular box that is aligned with the stage of the opera. Together they form an elongated space that opens up, through large stage doors, onto the public square. This space is a prototype space that invites new kinds of events, art forms and links potentially urban events like festivals to staged performances of various kinds. The stage connects with an experimental theatre to become a prototype stage that opens up to the urban square. The square becomes a field of potential performances initiated in the opera building. The façade becomes the proscenium plane. In the opera people watch the stage, in the music theatre the space of watching and acting is one, outside, on the square, people become actors themselves.

← The public space and the auditorium: an exchange of musical narratives

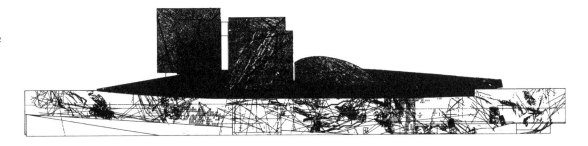

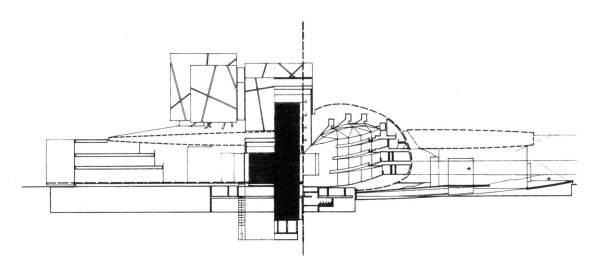

Elevation facing the public square: a glass façade with light installations; centre, access doors to the combined stages of the opera and musical theatre; and view of the pneumatic roof that forms the ground for the metacity of the stage tower and the rehearsal rooms

Split section: left, production spaces, backstage areas; right, separation plane between production spaces and public areas, auditorium, lobby

Steel model of striated spaces: the echo chambers

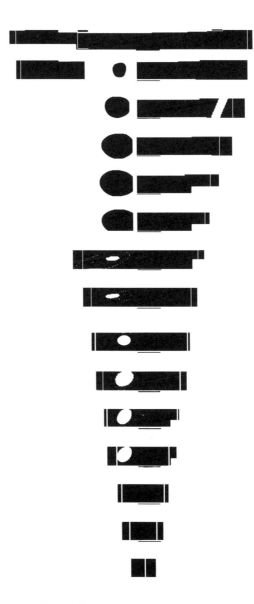

Echo chambers: top half, lobby and auditorium opera, bottom half, entrance to
experimental music theatre, centre line, prototype stage space

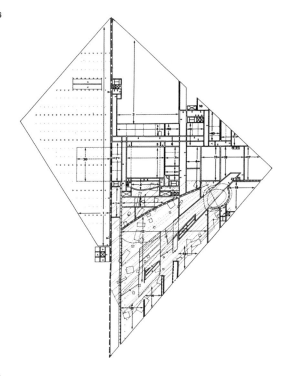

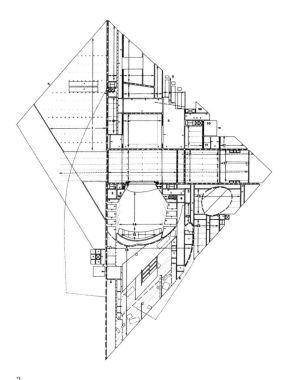

1

2

1   Technical spaces lower part of lobby, ramp leading to entrance of
    experimental music theatre
2   Upper lobby entrances from the street and public square, prototype stage
    space which includes the experimental music theatre

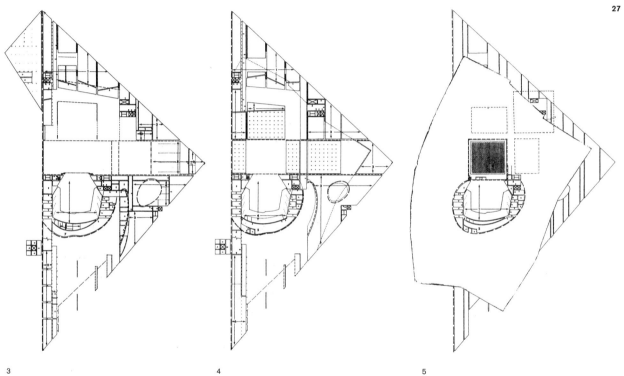

3

4

5

3 Void lobby, café (steps), production space, opera

4 Auditorium, restaurant and café

5 Pneumatic roof, top auditorium, stage tower

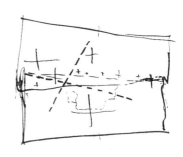

Prado Museum, Madrid

The Prado is one of the most incredibly beautiful, and moving art collections anywhere. It contains the *Gardens of Earthly Delights* by Bosch, the strange game of reversals in *Las Meninas* by Velasques, the gentle cloth-like landscapes by El Greco, but also the *Annunciation* by Fra Angelico – an angel telling Mary that she will conceive, facing her across a virtual divide projected onto the picture plane by an architectural element.

Prado means soft meadow, like the skin of the hill next to the medieval city of Madrid. The Museum sits on a fold between this hill and the city. The project lifts this skin up, extends it and folds it over to create a soft bed for the original Prado and the church behind it, and creates three public surfaces that link museum and city: the public square on top, the shaded courtyard with the restaurant under the top fold, and the large interior agora, the new entrance space underneath the lower fold, leading into the original Prado building and connecting the various extensions to each other. The Prado building now sits on an Urban Cloth, somewhat like a jewel. But this cloth is a multi-layered public space that becomes a centre for an urban micro-region while restructuring the topology of an urban landscape. The Urban Cloth forms the new frontage for the church of St Jeronimo, one of the most important churches in Spain. It is a space for ceremony. This top level is punctuated by a series of prismatic objects and geometric cut outs, these are rooms of light, or light crystals. Some of these are the new entrances, on the south and the north side. They lead to a large space, the Agora. This is a public space underneath the folds of the cloth. The light crystals bring light into this space, they also provide the structural system. The Agora has slopes that lead down to the centre, where there are public facilities, shops, and the entrances to the extension and the original building. This is entered underneath the inner fold, a kind of giant wing, from where escalators rise towards the first floor of the Prado. The Agora provides all the facilities that the Prado is currently lacking. But the folded structure as a whole creates a set of urban spaces that can be experienced in radically different ways: the top surface a space of ceremony, urban events, but also of heat and exposure. The middle space is shaded and sheltered, the inside space a vast room, with the knife of the retaining wall forming an inner façade facing the interior fold. The topology of the Urban Cloth is like that of a butterfly fold. There is a point near the middle where the visitor can cross over from the top surface and enter a slope that gradually becomes the shaded space underneath the exterior fold.

← Main entrance court (north) of the Prado Museum with folded cloth and the 'stitching' of functions

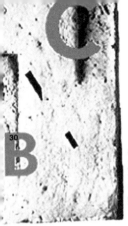

Prado, the 'soft skin of the earth', folded into a multi-layered public space, cushioning the original Prado building

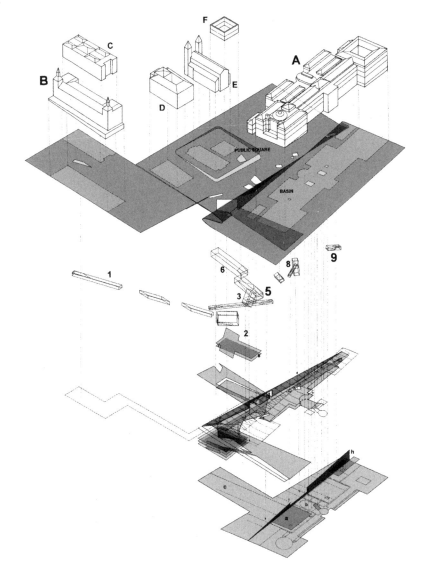

A Juan de Villanueva Building
   (Museo del Prado)

B Army Museum Building

C Cason del Buen Retiro Building

D Royal Academy of Spanish Language

E San Jeronimo el Real Parish Church

F Cloister of San Jeronimo el Real
   Parish Church

1 Stretch: underground exhibition halls
   connecting to buildings B-C-D

2 Repose: garden court

3 Weave: direct access to the café

4 Light well

5 Cross-over: main entrance

6 Assembly hall

7 Condense: computer communication

8 Tunnel: public access to toilets

9 Exit: south entrance

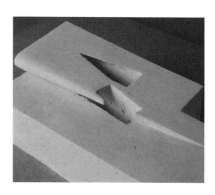

← View of the extension from the main (north) entrance to the south entrance
along the upper platform fronting the church of St Jeronimo
View of light chambers

View into the shaded outside space underneath the upper fold, restaurant and
café terrace
South entrance of Prado

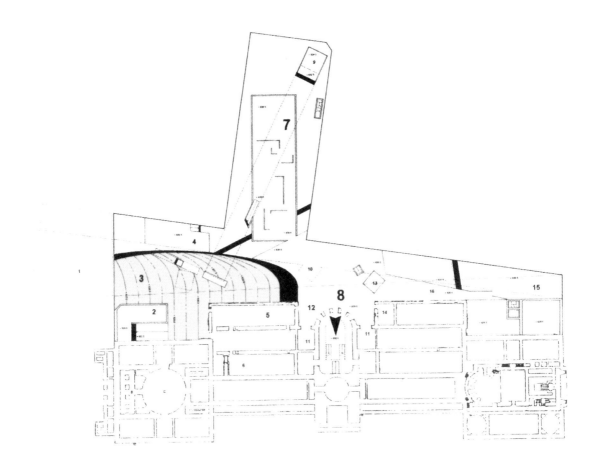

1 Garden/north entrance court

2 Restaurant/café with terrace on
   lower part of fold

3 Group reception/stitch
   connecting upper Agora to:

4 Main entrance/inner part of
   Agora and new galleries

5 Temporary exhibition hall/
   contemporary art gallery

6 Extension gallery/lobby

7 Seminar room

8 Lecture hall/auditorium

9 Digitised information post

10 Computerisation and
   communications department

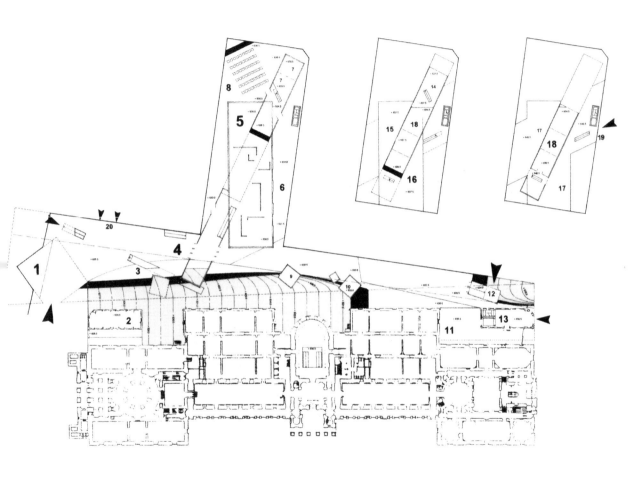

11 Restoration workshop

12 South entrance

13 Loading bay/goods entrance

14 Friends of the Prado Foundation

15 Royal trusteeship of the Prado Museum

16 Management of the Prado Museum

17 Administration and management areas

18 Assembly room

19 Staff entrance

20 Potential entrance to pedestrian subway

Ottakringer Brewery, Vienna

The Ottakringer Brewery is transforming its manufacturing processes and has therefore the chance to condense its production facilities in the site it occupies. It has proposed to the city of Vienna that the space coming free would mainly be used for public facilities with some housing and office spaces. The area where the Ottakringer Brewery is situated lacks a variety of public facilities, such as cinemas and a market. It also lacks a centre that has a clear identity. The project consists of a large landform, a hill that is visible as a landmark between the hills of the Wienerwald and St Stephan's Dome. It is made from large scale roof segments that each contain or cover distinct sets of programmes. Together they form a spherical segment. The main architectural configuration, apart from the sphere, is a cross embedded into the existing context, in part being anchored and positioned by the surrounding buildings. Over this cross another cross is placed but this cross is rotated by several degrees. This cross is also positioned by the existing buildings. The space between the crosses forms the main public space and creates a new set of streets within the site of the Brewery. The arms of the two crosses form cuts into the spherical segment. These cuts are the main façades of the building. All entrances and connections weave through these cuts. The roof slides over a set of existing buildings, leaving some features visible above its horizon. These features, the roof turret of the old headquarters of the brewery, parapets of an old storage building, become elements of the spherical landscape

of the roof, a large public space. The quadrants have different functions: NW is a brewery museum suspended above the older courtyards of the Brewery, NE is a complex of cinemas and other leisure facilities, SE is a large covered market that can double as venue for outdoor concerts and other performances, SW is a new set of offices for the Brewery. The edge of the market square is formed by a wall of housing and offices. The quadrants relate each in a specific way to global, national and local conditions. They each have different time cycles and time occupation rhythms. The architectural principle of this project is extremely simple: its form is a cross on the map and a sphere pushing through the skin of the earth, appearing as a hill on the horizon. But these two elements together create enough complexity to accommodate a phased construction process and the accommodation and interlinking of a variety of programmes combined with a vast open air public space. Simple forms have the power to be diagrammatic in organisation, and iconic in perception. They can organise and regulate complexity, and yet become identifiable and symbolic.

← Public Space as Omphalos, the restaurant as playground

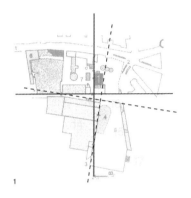
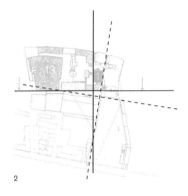
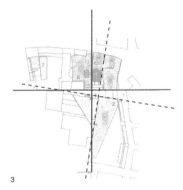
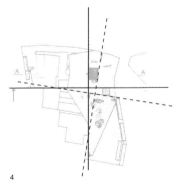

New public spaces and the interconnections formed by two rotated squares

1 Street level: left, remaining production spaces of the brewery, centre, entrances to new cultural facilities, bottom right, large market and performance space and public housing

2 Brewery, offices and, centre, cultural facilities

3 The Omphalos skin: from left, clockwise, museum of brewery, cinema complex, market hall roof, new offices brewery

4 Roof view: small objects on roofscape, sunken restaurant terrace in top of existing building

Formation of the Omphalos: meeting between Vienna and a small Earth

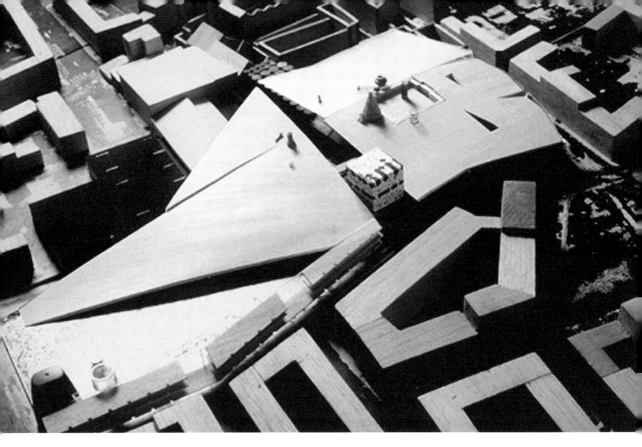

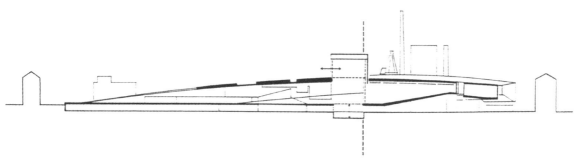

Top: view of Omphalos skin, with large market square at bottom
Bottom: section through market hall, stage tower and cinema space

→ New street with suspended stage tower of the outdoor performance space and
the new façade formed by the roof spanning over the former headquarter
building of the brewery, the storage silos and production facilities

42

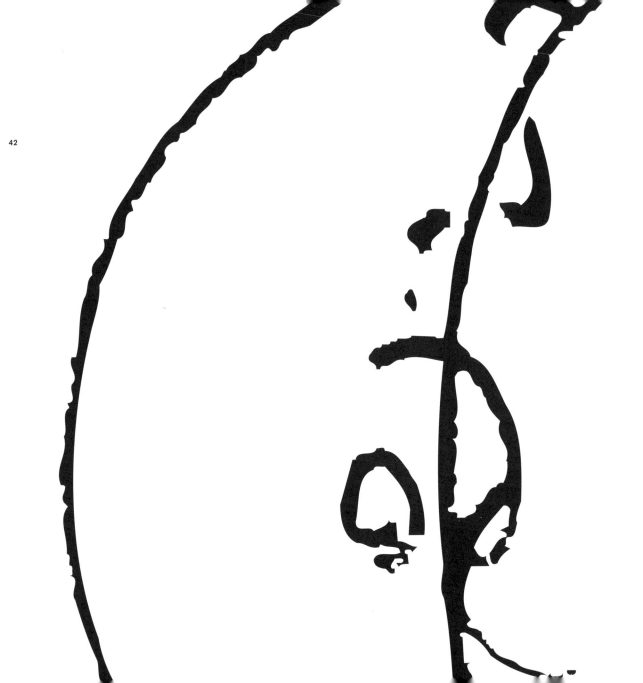

Meridian Walk, London

When the Millennium Dome was conceived and built
the time seemed ripe to propose alternative projects
that would both have a high symbolic character and
have an impact on the city. But, removing the aim of
showing the *zeitgeist* – an overview of our society and
the state of the art of many parts of that society – it is
possible to develop projects that use their symbolic
power to initiate real effects in specific parts of London.

What if one could walk a part of the Meridian, what if
this walk becomes a cross-section of London? What
does it mean to walk a line that is an international
marker of the measurement of time, and a national
symbol of scientific discovery and global expansion?
What if the creation of this walk creates conflicts of all
kinds – local conflicts, management problems,
conceptual conflicts, institutional, legal, political
conflicts – conflicts that need negotiations between
local and global partners, negotiations about the right
and possibility to walk the line, and about contingent
conflicts that can only be addressed by this configuration
of partners? Then this walk, or even its declared
intention, becomes an urban planning tool, a device
with which to change existing situations, a tool with
which to tackle problems indirectly that cannot be
dealt with in a direct manner.

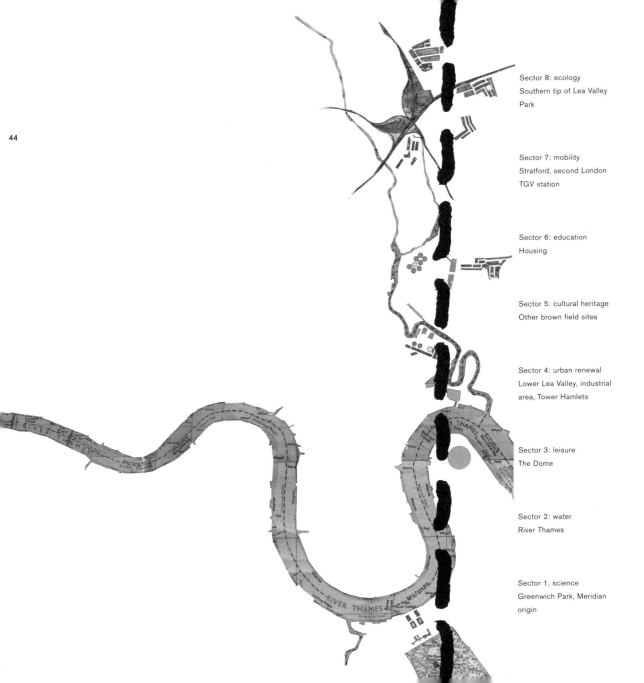

44

Sector 8: ecology
Southern tip of Lea Valley
Park

Sector 7: mobility
Stratford, second London
TGV station

Sector 6: education
Housing

Sector 5: cultural heritage
Other brown field sites

Sector 4: urban renewal
Lower Lea Valley, industrial
area, Tower Hamlets

Sector 3: leisure
The Dome

Sector 2: water
River Thames

Sector 1, science
Greenwich Park, Meridian
origin

1 Elderly Resident

He/she is unhappy with the change that the Meridian Walk may bring about to a familiar area. He/she uses the project to voice other local issues such as health concerns regarding contaminated land.

2 Owner of a newspaper shop

The owner has concerns regarding the future of his/her shop due to increased land value, and the possible moving in of large competition. He/she recognises the benefits of economic improvement and the potential to expand his/her small enterprise.

3 National Rivers Authority

The NRA Thames Region wants to focus on this part of the River Lea, in order to improve and protect the water environment.

4 Manager of British Gas

British Gas own local land which has been contaminated. They see the potential of the Meridian Walk in increasing the value of the land and the opportunities for publicity with the potential to increase their positive public relations both locally and nationally.

5 Lower Lee Partnership

Aiming to regenerate and revitalise this area, which was once a booming part of the national economy, through forming new partnerships.

A Project Manager

The project manager is an animator of the table, he/she ensures that a scenario will be developed by the actors and agents seated at the table and that they will abide by the game rules for the scenario.

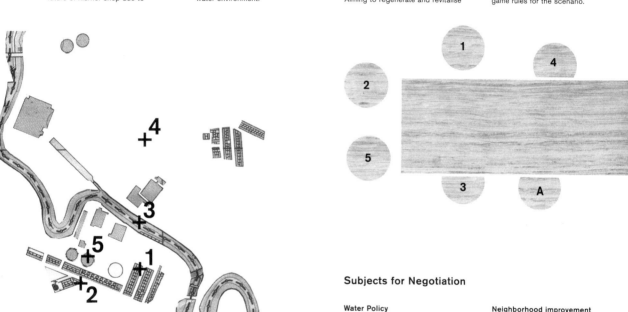

Subjects for Negotiation

Water Policy

How to manage a shift in water use from the transport industry to recreational ecological use within this part of the River Lea area? The effects of the change should bring about maximum benefits for all included.

Local economic development

In a climate of industrial change the needs of local enterprises in terms of advice, training, staff recruitment and business growth need to be addressed.

Neighborhood improvement

High unemployment has lead to increased crime rates and a sense of residential insecurity, and increased separation between communities. Practical solutions, which address these problems, need to be found.

Ground contamination

Land in the area is contaminated. Projects for purification are supported on a national and European level, however, sustainability needs to be built in on a local level.

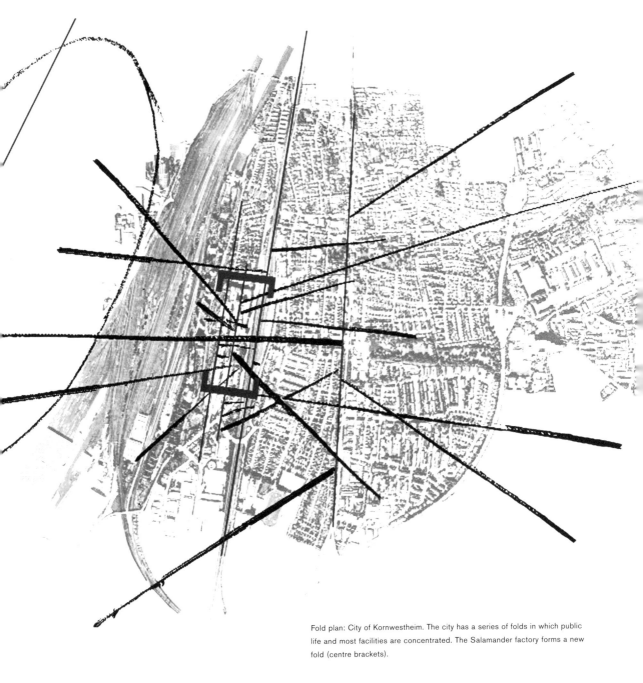

Fold plan: City of Kornwestheim. The city has a series of folds in which public life and most facilities are concentrated. The Salamander factory forms a new fold (centre brackets).

Salamander Factory: corporate change and dependent cities, Stuttgart Region

Kornwestheim, a town close to Stuttgart, has been the home of the Salamander shoe factory since the beginning of the twentieth century. The factory expanded several times, and is now an enormous complex of over 600 meters long. Since all production has been relocated the factory has stood empty. The project to restructure it originated in a workshop in which municipal authorities, factory managers and other actors took part. A short session of scenario games developed into a discussion about the potential of the factory complex in Kornwestheim. The current project developed from that discussion in cooperation with Salamander and the municipality of Kornwestheim. The project envisions the insertion of an infrastructural core into the cluster of existing factory buildings – an architectural and programmatic spine. This spine will act as a switching board for the new parties inhabiting the complex. The new infrastructure provides access and services, as well as providing a new face for the city. The city has been marred by this empty factory, as well as by a fast railway link running through it. That link, and the sheer size of the factory have resulted in a split in the town. Part of the project is to identify this split as being part of a series of folds running north-south through the town. Urban Folds form 'sutures' in a city, connecting devices as well as marks. The *Salamander Fold* becomes an architectural and infrastructural spine that plays a key role in the social, cultural and economic link-up of the city and the new urban complex of Salamander. The *Salamander Fold* turns the complex into a new city part, containing large-scale cultural activities: housing, start-up enterprises, retail, and several large companies. Apart from infrastructure it provides vertical public spaces in which clusters of companies are connected.

The *Salamander Fold* is a generator of change for the Salamander AG, the city with all its inhabitants and the Stuttgart Region. Besides creating effective change it is an urban prototype for other such situations in the region. As a model example it is an Urban Gallery for Kornwestheim, demonstrating innovative development of large-scale enterprises that have undergone radical change caused by global developments and are situated in dense urban contexts.

The *Salamander Fold* unfolds as follows:

a. The façade of the long spine forms a new face for Salamander and for the city as well. Thousands of people pass it daily on the S-Bahn and main line trains. The long spine building continues the architectural history of the sites' development. The façade also concludes a park that runs east-west through Kornwestheim.

b. Salamander's new spine is infrastructural, providing varied and flexible access to all existing parts of the complex, as well as forming a technical main channel into which new companies and other enterprises can literally 'plug-in'.

c. The spine stimulates continual change, adapting to new developments in the global market and trends in the social and cultural realm. It creates the means for economic futures and is also an instrument for shaping the urban identity of these futures.

d. It creates the means for an east-west weaving together of Kornwestheim, as well as an integration of the Salamander complex onto the city and region.

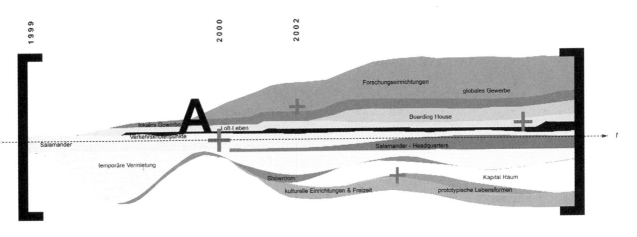

1. Corporate Identity

2. Salamander wird Stadt

3. Prototyp - Projekte

Visual business plan: construction and gradual occupation by programmes,
over a period of ten years

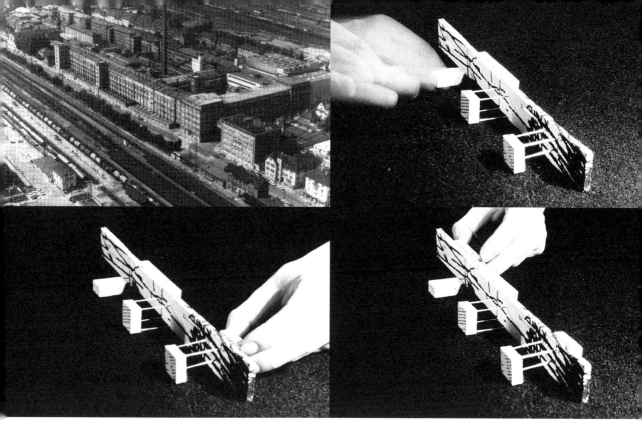

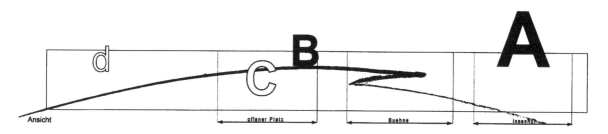

Ansicht

offener Platz   Buehne   Innenhof

Top: factory complex, infrastructural spine with plug-in programmes

Bottom: the Hill, a walkway through the spine

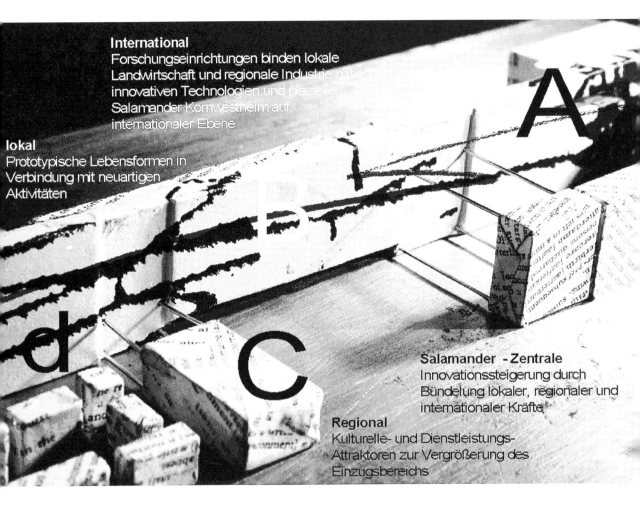

International
Forschungseinrichtungen binden lokale
Landwirtschaft und regionale Industrie mit
innovativen Technologien und plazieren
Salamander Kornwestheim auf
internationaler Ebene

lokal
Prototypische Lebensformen in
Verbindung mit neuartigen
Aktivitäten

Salamander - Zentrale
Innovationssteigerung durch
Bündelung lokaler, regionaler und
internationaler Kräfte

Regional
Kulturelle- und Dienstleistungs-
Attraktoren zur Vergrößerung des
Einzugsbereichs

The infrastructure forms a new façade towards the town centre, ending the Salamander Park, and facing the national railway line

A Salamander Centre: intensification of innovation by linking local, regional and global forces

B International: Research institutions combine local agriculture and regional industry with innovative technologies, putting Salamander and Kornwestheim on an international stage

C Cultural and service attractors increase the catchment area and increase the role of Salamander as new public space

D Local: Prototypical life forms intertwine with a programme of new events and actions

Spatial relations

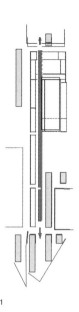

1

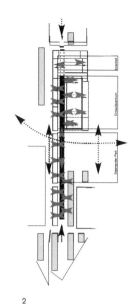

2

3

4

5

6

7

1 Spine: a core containing all technical and communication infrastructure,
additional building elements (grey)
2 New organisation of access points through the core
3 Spine and existing factory body
4 Programmatic knots serving both sides of the core

5 Large programmes attached to core
6 The core as gateway and threshold: urban activities weave through it
7 The core generates other programmes around the Salamander Factory
complex: public transport, restaurants, cultural activities, shops, an
extension of the central city park, foot bridges over the railway, etc.

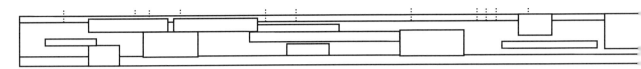

STUDIO   SMALL BUSINESS

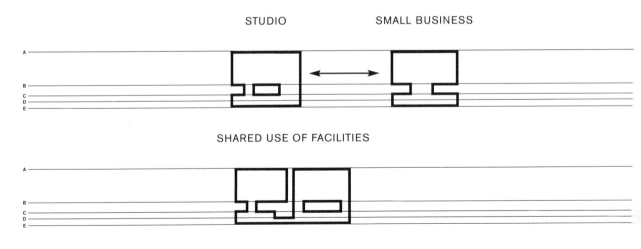

SHARED USE OF FACILITIES

Top: elevation of core

Inserted diagram: interlinking of programmes and spaces

Bottom: variations on the joining of private spaces and semi-public spaces

Lines:

A   Façade of original building

A/B Main spaces in the original building

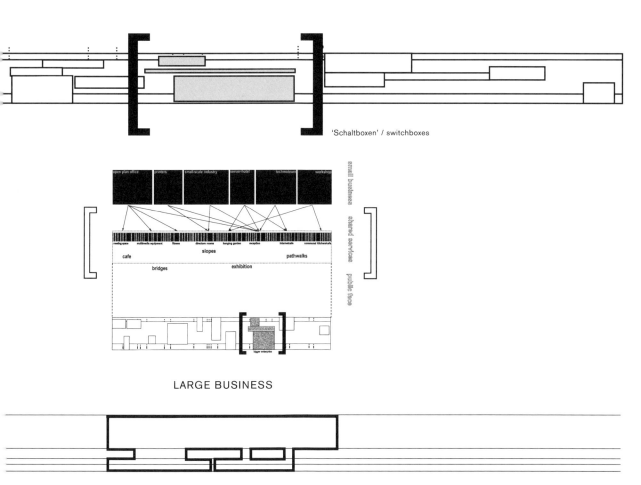

'Schaltboxen' / switchboxes

open plan office | printers | small-scale industry | server-hotel | techmoteum | workshop

small business

shared services

reading space | multimedia equipment | fitness | directors rooms | hanging garden | reception | internetcafé | communal kitchen/café

slopes

cafe | pathwalks

bridges | exhibition

public face

bigger enterprise

LARGE BUSINESS

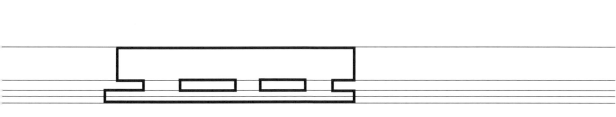

B/C Voids between original building and new core building

C/D Spaces for facilities and the walkway

D/E Entry spaces, public spaces, together forming the 'Switchboxes'

E Skin and façade of the new core, with projection surfaces and light installations

Municipal Museum of Contemporary Art, Rome

The project houses the municipal art collection, but also aims at being a gallery for contemporary art. Since the art of curation is changing rapidly, it is important to create gallery facilities that are programmable in many different ways. It is also important that large exhibitions can co-exist with smaller exhibitions that are woven into the larger one. The project consists of an existing building and an extension. The existing building has a galleria, an open air space covered by a large glass roof. The structure of the new complex consists of three main elements: A. a long, multi-programmable space that combines the galleria space with the black-box space inside the new gallery, which together forms a kind of interior street; B. service walls, they contain the infrastructure including stairs and elevators. In the entrance lobby a large service wall is suspended by a wire mesh structure from the ceiling. This suspended translucent wall system provides a route from the lobby into the gallery floor, but also contains an independent route through the building, from the galleria to the lower street level garden; C. the roof is a public square, formed like a game board, a grid from which the multi-programmable particle spaces are suspended.

The platform, an elevated square, links the celestial and cultural space of Rome to local activities and new practices of art curation like outdoor performances and multimedia projections. The platform is the largest of the curatable spaces that is both museum space as well as public, urban space.

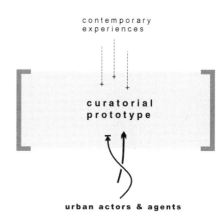

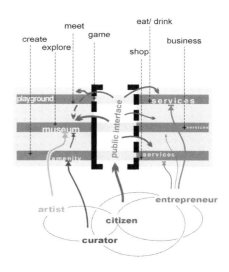

← Top level museum: public square and playground, part of the curation prototype

Curatorial strategy

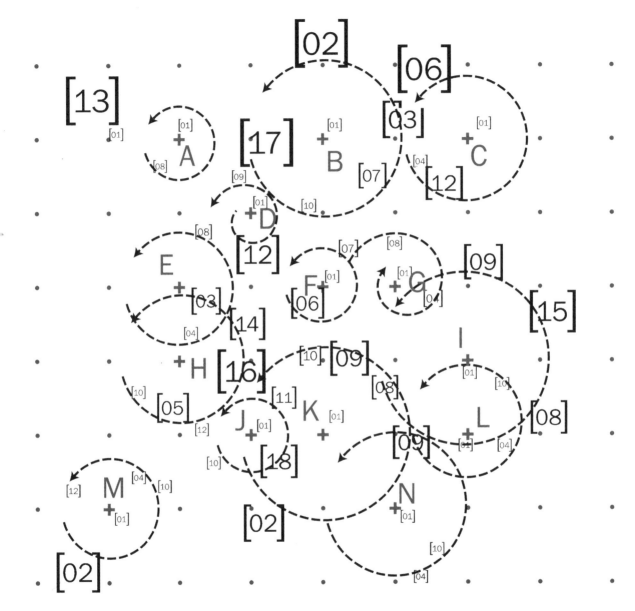

New Suburb, Høje Taastrup, Copenhagen

In Spring 2000 a competition for a new concept for the suburb took place in Denmark with two sites, one of them near Copenhagen. This project, which won the second prize, proposes a dynamic masterplan on the basis of the Urban Gallery as it was proposed in the book *Urban Flotsam*. This planning tool has four drivers: a database of existing and emergent conditions, a prototype bank, negotiation structures to develop scenarios, and action plans to implement the scenarios. The project assumes that there is a virtual space, the Urban Gallery, in which the prototypes link very different programmes together across the specific floors of the gallery in order to maximise potential and minimise conflicts.

How to apply the Urban Gallery? The project proposes the conception of a game board as a vast, apparently brutal, but very simple device to both embed the Urban Gallery as a planning mechanism in the site, and to turn this whole mechanism into a public space. The game board and its grid points are like a common, they have public values. Each grid point is a potential anchor and sign for a community. These communities consist of existing elements, housing, a church, sports facilities, which are often modified and in most cases combined with new programmes. The communities are both mutations and new identities. Urban Prototypes are introduced to develop a dynamic condition for each community and to introduce innovative conditions.

In the typically decentralised zones of suburbia this is a recipe for the formation of new communities, each with their own identity and yet sharing common facilities and space. The recipe creates a new topology for urban dynamics and a practice of planning that combines clear form – the gameboard, the spiralling growth of the communities – with unpredictable developments – the interlinking of the communities. Three main aspects underly the proposal: designing new life forms for suburbs, stimulating dynamic growth, sustaining a balanced urban environment

The method balances an evaluation of the existing with a nurturing of the new. It is a game with strict rules but infinite possibilities. The combination of centres, programmes, prototypes and communities create incubators of new urban life forms. The key to these new life forms are the prototypes. Urban Prototypes are generating complexity, they inject centrifugal growth in each centre and initiate new clustering of urban programmes. They introduce innovative projects related to lifestyle, culture, ecology, land use, management, financing and government.

The project introduces a planning mechanism that mixes landscape and dense urban environments, production facilities and leisure, live and work, and yet it aims at clarifying the spatial conditions of these functions, to create clear and identifiable public spaces that articulate both local qualities as well as interacting with global forces and trends. The project for Høje Taastrup is itself a prototype for a new form of organisation of a masterplan. The time based space of the Urban Gallery is a new type of public space.

← Gameboard with Centres (A, B, C, etc.), Prototypes ([01], [02], [03], etc.) and Communities (spirals)

58

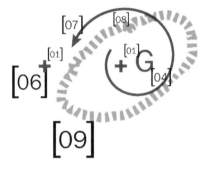

DNA code for community G, main components of its dynamics   → Main plan of the Høje Taastrup new suburb City

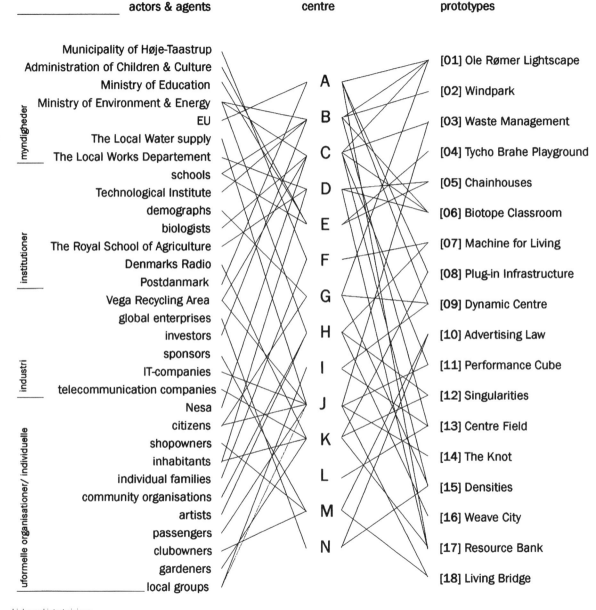

actors & agents	centre	prototypes

actors & agents

myndigheder
- Municipality of Høje-Taastrup
- Administration of Children & Culture
- Ministry of Education
- Ministry of Environment & Energy
- EU
- The Local Water supply
- The Local Works Departement

institutioner
- schools
- Technological Institute
- demographs
- biologists
- The Royal School of Agriculture
- Denmarks Radio
- Postdanmark
- Vega Recycling Area

industri
- global enterprises
- investors
- sponsors
- IT-companies
- telecommunication companies
- Nesa

uformelle organisationer/ individuelle
- citizens
- shopowners
- inhabitants
- individual families
- community organisations
- artists
- passengers
- clubowners
- gardeners
- local groups

centre

A B C D E F G H I J K L M N

prototypes

- [01] Ole Rømer Lightscape
- [02] Windpark
- [03] Waste Management
- [04] Tycho Brahe Playground
- [05] Chainhouses
- [06] Biotope Classroom
- [07] Machine for Living
- [08] Plug-in Infrastructure
- [09] Dynamic Centre
- [10] Advertising Law
- [11] Performance Cube
- [12] Singularities
- [13] Centre Field
- [14] The Knot
- [15] Densities
- [16] Weave City
- [17] Resource Bank
- [18] Living Bridge

Links and intertwinings

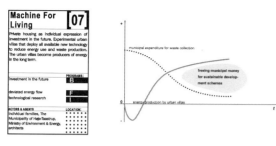

Machine For Living `07`

Private housing as individual expression of investment in the future. Experimental urban villas that deploy all available new technology to reduce energy use and waste production. The urban villas become producers of energy in the long term.

	PROGRAMS:
investment in the future	B
deviated energy flow	F
technological research	I

ACTORS & AGENTS:	LOCATION:
Individual families, The Municipality of Høje-Taastrup, Ministry of Environment & Energy, architects	·· ··· ·· ··

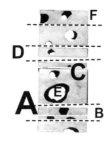

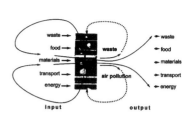

input   output

Performance Cube `11`

Community center with a virtual cube above it - an open 3D-stage with at least one horizontal and one vertical plane accomodating possible formal and informal events. A high platform suspended between heaven and earth provides the experience to touch the sky and view the horizon.

	PROGRAMS:
cultural identity	B
between heaven and earth	E
cultural exchange	F
local production and mediation	I

ACTORS & AGENTS:	LOCATION:
citizens, artists, local groups, sponsors, The Municipality of Høje-Taastrups Department of Culture	·· ··· ·· ··

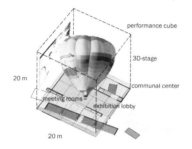

Singularities `12`

Cuts in the formless flotsam of suburbia. They define valleys, mountains, thresholds, doorways, views and edges: a phenomenological morphology of the center field.

	PROGRAMS:
collective identity	B
social subjects	E
cultural production	I

ACTORS & AGENTS:	LOCATION:
landscape architects, artists, inhabitants	·· ··· ·· ··

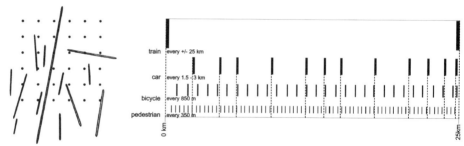

Densities `15`

How to create and maintain diversity in the suburb? A set of rules and the allocation of maxima and minima of density creates a differentiated landscape of densities. They define an outline for future development and yet provide an adaptive and open growth.

	PROGRAMS:
tops and valleys	E
legal management	I

ACTORS & AGENTS:	LOCATION:
local city planners, investors, Ministry of Environment & Energy, demographs	·· ··· ·· ··

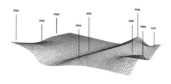

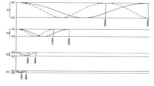

Samples of prototype boxes outlining their programme, and specific prototypes

Credits

Apeiron, Berlin, 1988
Raoul Bunschoten with Davis Evans assisted by Stella
Moy, and Juan d'Ornellas, Chris Flannery, Christel
Wanten, Iris Gazenfeld, Isabella Binet and Jörg Röhrig
(model)
Developed for the exhibition, Berlin: *Denkmal oder
Denkmodell*, Kunsthalle Berlin, 1988

**Constantini Museum for South American Art,
Buenos Aires, 1998**
Raoul Bunschoten, Eva Castro, Alessandra Papiri, Jörg
Röhrig, Jason Coleman, Takuro Hoshino, Dagmar Stirch,
Ove Arup and Partners, structural and mechanical
engineers
International Design Competition, 1998

Welsh National Opera, Cardiff, 1994
Raoul Bunschoten with Takuro Hoshino, Joost Grootens,
Jeroen van Mechelen and Shi Chieh Lu
International Design Competition, 1994

Prado Museum, Madrid, 1995
Raoul Bunschoten, Juan d'Ornellas, Takuro Hoshino,
Jason Coleman and Catrien Coppens (model)
International Design Competition, 1995

Omphalos, Ottakringer Brewery, Vienna, 1996
Raoul Bunschoten, Mathis Güller, Takuro Hoshino,
International Design Competition, 1996

Meridian Walk, London,1998
Takuro Hoshino, Raoul Bunschoten, Julie Parret and
Amy Plant
Proposal to the London Arts Board, 1998

**Salamander Factory: corporate change and
dependent cities, Stuttgart Region, 2000**
Raoul Bunschoten, Manuela Aberle, Petra Marquc,
Andrea Adis, Shai Akram and Thomas Kovari
In collaboration with the city of Kornwestheim and
Salamander AG.

Municipal Museum of Contemporary Art, Rome, 2001
Raoul Bunschoten, Shuman Basar, Patrick Lam, Parag
Raj Sharma, Franz Sdoutz, Michael Katsibas, Dion Ho,
Jeong-der Ho, Harald Keijer, Jonas Upton Hansen and
Alvin Yip
International Design Competition, 2001

The New Suburb, Høje Taastrup, Copenhagen, 2000
Raoul Bunschoten, Petra Marquc, Tordis Berstrand,
Charles Karasik, Gary Doherty, Annette Chu, Gilles
Chan, Jonas Upton Hansen, Michael Katsibas and
Mimi Mollica (photographs)

Book cover:
**From *Migrations*, a series of projects for Arnhem,
the Netherlands, 1993**
Raoul Bunschoten, Takuro Hoshino, Catrien Coppens

Colophon

© 2002 Black Dog Publishing Limited and the author
Produced by Duncan McCorquodale
Designed by Joost Grootens
Photographs by Hélène Binet
Printed in the European Union

Acknowledgements
Gary Doherty, Dirk Lellau, Tordis Berstand, Beata Teresa
Wroblewska, Anne Katrine Hornemann and Johannes
Pedersen for assembling the materials for this book.
Members of CHORA, past and present. Students from
the Architectural Association and the Berlage Institute.

Black Dog Publishing Limited
5 Ravenscroft Street
London E2 7SH
tel. +44 (0)20 7613 1922
fax. +44 (0)20 7613 1944
email: info@bdp.demon.co.uk

ISBN: 1 901033 76 7